A Drop in the Ocean

DAILY INSPIRATIONS FOR BEING

A Drop in the Ocean

BY DR. DAIN HEER

For questions, please contact:
Access Consciousness Publishing
406 Present Street
Stafford, TX 77477 USA
accessconsciousnesspublishing.com

AC|P

Welcome!

These are inspirations for possibility that really speak for themselves.

May they brighten your day. Your week. Your month. And hopefully your life.

Enjoy,

Dain

Ps. With huge gratitude to my sister, Sarah Grandinetti, who originally compiled these for me as a wonderful Christmas present that I wanted to share with you.

THE DIFFERENCE YOU ACTUALLY ARE IS NOT DEFINABLE.

DAIN HEER

ACCESS CONSCIOUSNESS

YOU DON'T HAVE TO
BE PERFECT TO
BE FUCKING PHENOMENAL

DAIN HEER

ALLOWANCE IS WHERE
TRUE CREATION EXISTS

DAIN HEER

Be the ask. Don't think the ask.

Dain Heer

With a background of silence, you can hear the whisper of awareness

DAIN HEER

THE REALITY YOU CREATE IS BASED ON THE QUESTIONS YOU ASK

DAIN HEER

BEYOND
THIS REALITY IS WHERE YOUR REALITY BEGINS

DAIN HEER

IF SOMETHING IS NOT YOURS,
YOU CANNOT CHANGE IT.
YOU CAN ONLY LET IT GO.

DAIN HEER

WHAT YOU DO NOT ACKNOWLEDGE, DOES NOT EXIST FOR YOU

DAIN HEER

IF YOU WANT TO CHANGE YOUR FUTURE, CHANGE YOUR CHOICES.

DAIN HEER

STRUGGLE IS WHAT YOU DO TO PROVE YOU DON'T
HAVE CHOICE

DAIN HEER

UNTIL YOU CHOOSE NOTHING CHANGES

DAIN HEER

CONSCIOUSNESS IS LIKE GOING TO THE GYM: CHOOSING IT ONCE ISN'T GONNA CHANGE MUCH. **CHOOSING IT CONSISTENTLY** CHANGES EVERYTHING

DAIN HEER

CREATION IS
THE BEST ANTIDOTE
TO BEING PATHETIC

DAIN HEER

EVERY DAY YOU HAVE JOY
IS A DAY YOU
CONTRIBUTE
TO THIS PLANET
BEING GREATER

- DAIN HEER -

IT'S YOUR DEFINITION OF SOMETHING THAT CREATES IT AS REAL

DAIN HEER

DON'T FIGHT THIS REALITY
CREATE A NEW ONE

DAIN HEER

IF YOU'RE GOING TO HAVE SOMETHING DIFFERENT YOU HAVE TO BE WILLING TO BE DIFFERENT

DAIN HEER

EVERY PROBLEM IS
A POSSIBILITY IN DISGUISE.

DAIN HEER

DON'T FIGHT THIS REALITY, CHOOSE YOURS

DAIN HEER

THE EARTH DOES NOT REQUIRE SAVING.

IT REQUIRES

empowering.

DAIN HEER

THE EASIEST JOB YOU WILL EVER HAVE

is the one you were born to do

DAIN HEER

CONSCIOUSNESS IS
THE MOST ELEGANT FORCE FOR CHANGE IN
THE WORLD.
It will never give
YOU ANYTHING YOU CAN'T HANDLE.
IT WILL NEVER LET YOU DOWN.
CONSCIOUSNESS WILL NEVER NOT HAVE YOUR BACK.

Dain Heer

Every single change **that you experience** is the doorway to something greater, no matter how it looks

Dain Heer

- IN THE FACE OF HAPPINESS, -
EVERYTHING IS POSSIBLE

DAIN HEER

ACCESS
CONSCIOUSNESS

IN THE FACE OF JUDGMENT TURN IT UP

DAIN HEER

knowing is not solid.
it is like a feather touch.

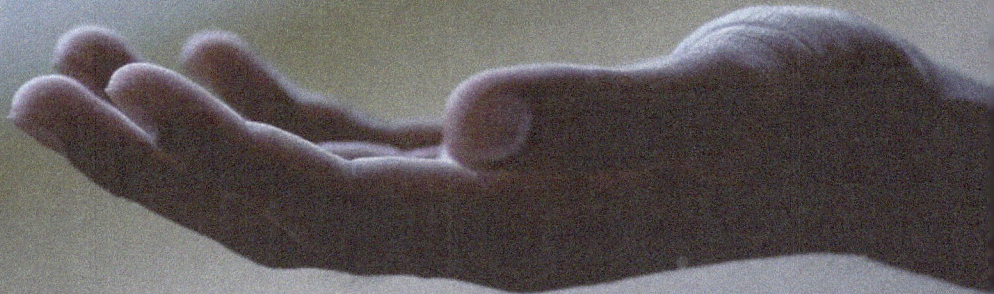

DAIN HEER

FOLLOW WHAT'S LIGHT FOR YOU, EVEN IF NOBODY GETS IT

DAIN HEER

- YOU CAN'T SEE THE FUTURE -

BUT YOU CAN BE THE FUTURE

DAIN HEER

YOU ARE THE GIFT THIS WORLD HAS BEEN WAITING FOR

DAIN HEER

THE MORE GRATEFUL YOU ARE FOR PEOPLE, THE MORE REASONS THEY WILL GIVE YOU TO BE GRATEFUL FOR THEM.

DAIN HEER

GRATITUDE IS THE
KEY TO THE
KINGDOM OF POSSIBILITY

Dain Heer

HAPPINESS IS A CHOICE
YOU HAVE TO MAKE

DAIN HEER

If we truly desire to create a different world, our only task and most important task is to get happy!

— Dain Heer

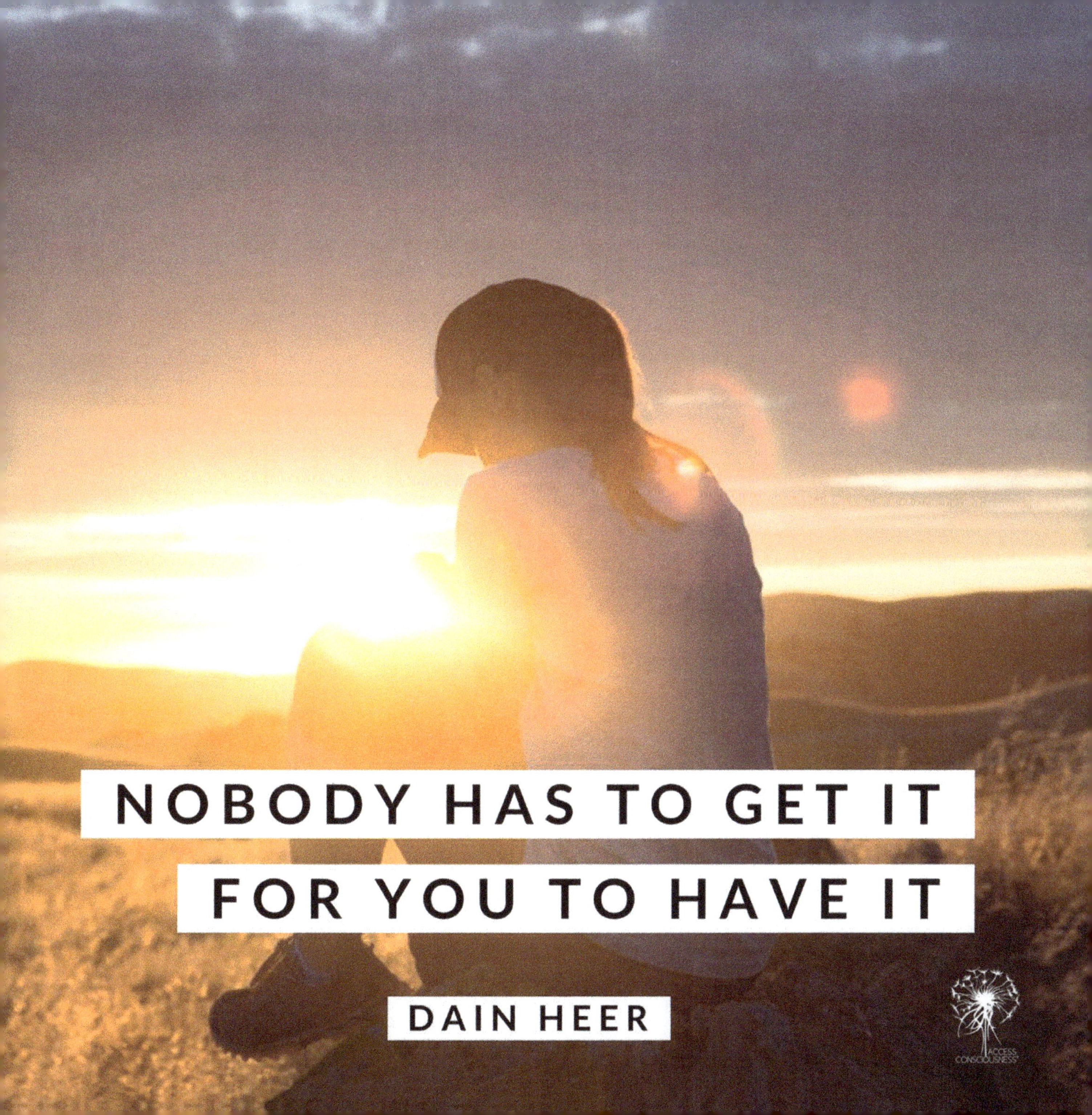
NOBODY HAS TO GET IT
FOR YOU TO HAVE IT
DAIN HEER

Joy is only POSSIBLE WHEN YOU EMBRACE HOW IMPERFECT YOU ARE AND ACTUALLY LOVE IT

DAIN HEER

GRATITUDE CHANGES EVERYTHING. JUDGEMENT CHANGES NOTHING.

DAIN HEER

THE KEY TO NEVER BEING DISAPPOINTED IS NEVER HAVING EXPECTATIONS.

DAIN HEER

EVERY LIE YOU
LET GO OF,
MAKES IT EASIER TO
DESTROY THE NEXT ONE

DAIN HEER

LIFE'S WAY TOO LONG
TO NOT LOVE LIVING IT!

DAIN HEER

Looking through **THE EYES OF THIS** REALITY IS A RECIPE FOR **THE WRONGNESS OF YOU**

Dain Heer

YOU CAN'T LOSE
SOMETHING YOU ARE

DAIN HEER

MAGIC IS THE ART
of creating
YOUR LIFE FROM TOTAL EASE.

Dain Heer

FROM A SPACE OF
OF CONSCIOUSNESS,
MIRACLES AND MAGIC ARE PRAGMATIC

DAIN HEER

Most people would MORE WILLINGLY *hold in place the lie that* STICKS THEM THAN CHOOSE THE FREEDOM THEY CAN'T DEFINE.

DAIN HEER

THE NEED TO BE RIGHT DESTROYS.

DAIN HEER

- NOBODY IS VALUABLE ENOUGH -
TO MAKE YOURSELF
WRONG FOR

DAIN HEER

WHAT IF NOTHING IN YOUR

life were an **OBLIGATION,** *and everything were a choice?*

DAIN HEER

THE ONLY THING THAT IS GOING TO CHANGE YOUR LIFE IS MAKING DIFFERENT CHOICES

DAIN HEER

THERE IS NO PATH.
ONLY CHOICE.

DAIN HEER

You being everything you are
IS NOT AN INVALIDATION TO OTHERS,
IT'S AN INSPIRATION TO OTHERS!

Dain Heer

If you truly would like to change
THE FACE OF THE PLANET WE CURRENTLY LIVE ON TO ONE OF POSSIBILITIES FROM ONE OF IMPOSSIBILITIES... GET HAPPY.

DAIN HEER

ANY POINT OF VIEW
WE TAKE BECOMES
THE REALITY
———— WE LIVE ————

DAIN HEER

WHEN YOU LOOK FROM BEYOND THIS REALITY,

ALL YOU SEE IS POSSIBILITIES

Dain Heer

POTENCY IS THE CAPACITY TO CREATE CHANGE IN ANYTHING

DAIN HEER

To fight,
you have to think
you are powerless

Dain Heer

PRESENCE IS THE ONLY THING THAT CAN CHANGE YOUR PROBLEM INTO A POSSIBILITY

DAIN HEER

RIGHTNESS IS
NEVER FREEDOM.
RIGHTNESS IS ALWAYS A
prison of your
OWN MAKING

Dain Heer

EVERY PROBLEM YOU HAVE IS

SOMETHING FROM
THIS REALITY

EVERY POSSIBILITY YOU HAVE IS

SOMETHING FROM
_____

BEYOND THIS REALITY

Dain Heer

QUESTION ALWAYS TAKES SOLIDITY AND TURNS IT BACK INTO MOVEMENT

DAIN HEER

This reality cannot stop you from creating yours unless you fight it

Dain Heer

YOUR LIFE RIGHT NOW IS
A RESULT OF EVERYTHING
YOU'VE BEEN
ASKING FOR SHOWING UP.

DAIN HEER

RIGHTNESS IS
THE DEATH OF POSSIBILITY

DAIN HEER

IF WHAT YOU'VE BEEN ASKING FOR HASN'T SHOWN UP IT'S BECAUSE **YOUR ASK IS TOO SMALL**

DAIN HEER

SOMEBODY WHO JUDGES, JUDGES.
SOMEBODY WHO'S LOOKING
FOR A DIFFERENT
POSSIBILITY WILL
ASK YOU A QUESTION.

DAIN HEER

YOU ARE THE SOURCE FOR EVERYTHING THAT GETS CREATED IN YOUR LIFE

DAIN HEER

FROM A SPACE OF CONSCIOUSNESS, NOTHING THAT EVER OCCURS IS WRONG OR RIGHT

DAIN HEER

YOU ARE THAT SPARK
THAT GIVES
BIRTH TO
THE FIRE OF
POSSIBILITIES IF
YOU ARE WILLING TO
BE IT

DAIN HEER

THE DIFFERENCE THAT
YOU ARE IS THE GIFT

DAIN HEER

choice is the one
THING THAT
undoes mechanization

DAIN HEER

IF WE'RE GOING TO CREATE A DIFFERENT WORLD, WE HAVE TO CHOOSE TO BE DIFFERENT!

DAIN HEER

THE CHOICE
YOU MAKE TODAY CREATES
THE FUTURE YOU HAVE TOMORROW

DAIN HEER

THE ONLY PLACE
of total receiving
IS NO DEFINITION OF YOU

dain heer

You want to change something?
Undefine it.
-Dr. Dain Heer

STOP TRYING TO UNDERSTAND THE RULES. BREAK THEM.

DAIN HEER

UNTIL YOU CHOOSE THERE IS NO HOW

DAIN HEER

why
would you wait
until tomorrow?

dain heer

THE WILLINGNESS TO RECEIVE JUDGMENT IS ONE OF THE GREATEST GIFTS YOU CAN GIVE YOURSELF

DAIN HEER

IF YOU ONLY HAD ONE STEP
TO TAKE TODAY
TOWARDS WHAT
YOU WOULD LIKE
TO CREATE
OR CHANGE IN THE FUTURE
WHAT WOULD THAT BE?

DAIN HEER

THE ACTION YOU TAKE TODAY CREATES

THE FUTURE YOU HAVE TOMORROW.

WHAT ACTION ARE YOU TAKING?

- DAIN HEER -

it's
your choice
that creates
the change

dain heer

Why a Drop in The Ocean?

When my sister Sarah picked the title for this book, she was inspired by one particular quote—one you haven't seen yet.

When you flip this last page, you will ...

That is the possibility I would like to leave you with.

And if you knew that to be true, for you, what would be possible that has never been possible before?

For all of us? :-)

Dain

WE ARE NOT EITHER THE DROP
OR THE OCEAN.
WE ARE THE DROP AND
THE OCEAN SIMULTANEOUSLY.

DAIN HEER

Dr. Dain Heer

Dr. Dain Heer is a bestselling author, entrepreneur and internationally renowned speaker. He is a co-creator and leading facilitator of Access Consciousness, a personal development modality practiced in around 175 countries. Originally raised in the ghettos of Los Angeles and trained as a chiropractor, Dr. Heer is also the co-founder of a diverse range of businesses around the world.

A conscious and creative thought leader with a profound understanding of the power of personal creation, Dr. Heer draws upon his background and unique perspective to facilitate positive change in the world, and empower people from every culture, country, age and social strata to create the life, money, and relationships they desire.

www.drdainheer.com
www.accessconsciousness.com

www.ingramcontent.com/pod-product-compliance
Lightning Source LLC
Chambersburg PA
CBHW041559260326
41914CB00011B/1321